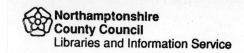

All about you

Who are you?

Jillian Powell

Wayland

All *about you*

Where did you come from?
Who are you?
Who are your family?
Who are your friends?

Picture Acknowledgements
The publishers would like to thank the following for allowing
their photographs to be reproduced in this book: Bryan and Cherry
Alexander 6 (centre below text box), 22 (below); Bruce Coleman Ltd
13 (Alain Compost/above left); Chris Fairclough Colour Library 12;
Reflections (Jennie Woodcock) 8, 9 (both), 13 (below left), 14, 25, 27;
Timothy Woodcock Library 10 (Steve Horsted/TWP), 15 (Tim Woodcock),
20 (Tim Woodcock/TWP), 24 (Tim Woodcock); Wayland Picture Library
6 (all except centre below text box), 11, 18, 27 (above); Tony
Stone Worldwide *cover*, 5 (Nicole Katano), 7 (Dale Durfee),
13 (above right/Don Smetzer), 16 (Chip Henderson), 17 (Don and
Pat Valenti), 21 (Andy Cox), 22 (above/Nicole Katano), 23 (Dale
Durfee), 28 (Ken Fisher), 29 (Jo Browne/Mick Smee); ZEFA *title
page,* 4, 18, 26.

Editor: Francesca Motisi
Series designer: Jean Wheeler

First published in 1993 by
Wayland (Publishers) Limited
61, Western Road, Hove
East Sussex, BN3 1JD England

© Copyright 1993 Wayland (Publishers) Limited

British Cataloguing in Publication Data
Powell, Jillian
Who are You?. – (All About You Series)
I. Title II. Series
305.23

ISBN 0-7502-0730-2

Typeset by Dorchester Typesetting Group Limited
Printed and bound by G. Canale and C.S.p.A., Turin, Italy

Contents

You are you. There is no one else quite like you in the world.

Have you ever thought what
makes you different from
everyone else?

You look different from anyone else. You have your own colour of hair, skin and eyes.

6

No one else has exactly your shape of face, or eyes, nose and mouth.

You may look a bit like your mum or dad, or like your brother or sister. Perhaps you have the same colour eyes or hair.

Twins look alike, but when you get to know them and look carefully, you can see differences.

You have your own name, your own voice and your own thoughts and ideas. You know what you like and dislike!

You may have a colour you like best. Which things do you choose because you like the colour?

Think about the clothes you wear. Are they different from your friends' clothes?

You like eating some foods and you don't like eating others! What is your **favourite** meal?

You have things which you
like doing. Perhaps you like
painting, or playing with a
favourite toy.

Sometimes you have to do things you don't like. What don't you like doing?

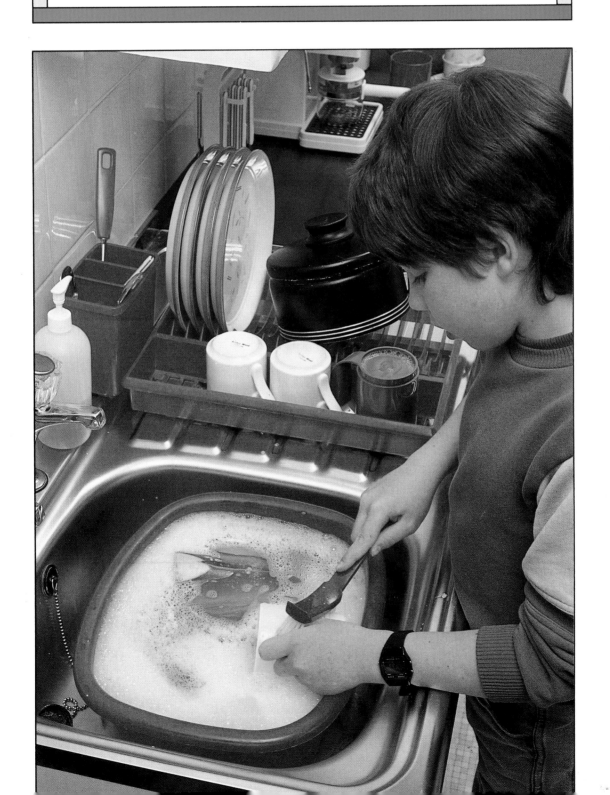

You are good at doing some things and not so good at others.

You might be good at running
or jumping, or using computers.

Your **brain** and your **five senses** help you learn new things all the time.

It can be fun learning new things.

You can do some things without thinking because you learned them when you were a baby.

You learned to smile and talk when you were a baby. You also learned to crawl then walk.

Some things make
you feel happy.

You feel happy when you are doing things you like, and when you are with people you like.

Some things make you feel
sad or scared.

Talking can make you feel better. Cuddling a toy, or stroking a pet can make you feel better too.

You are **special** to your family and to your friends, just as they are special to you.

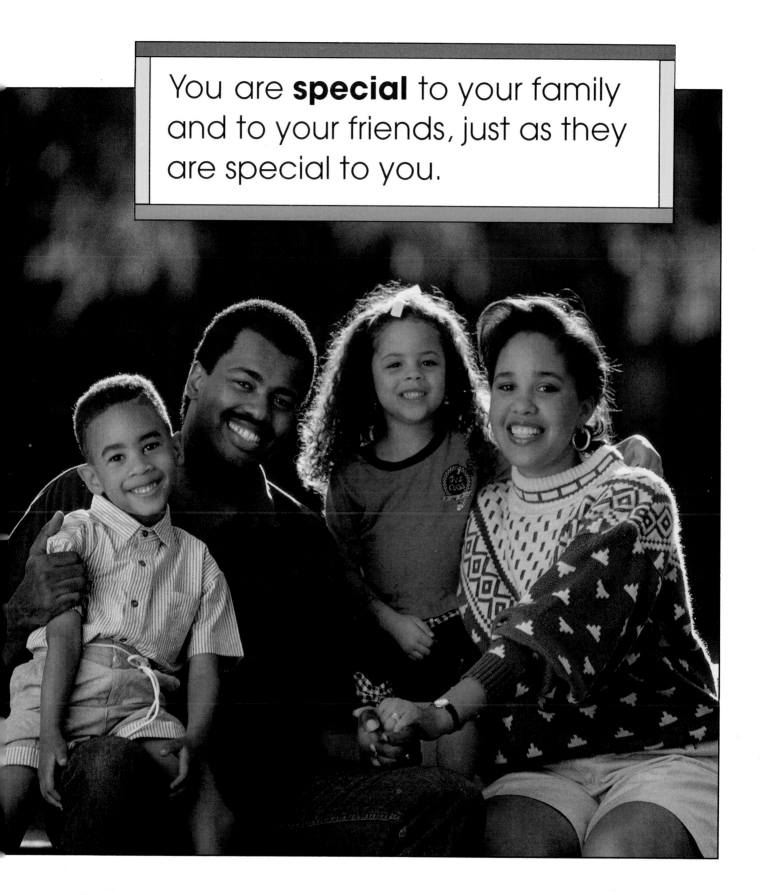

Notes for parents and teachers

Maths
- Gathering data about similarities and differences between children will provide many opportunities for number work, especially in the context of 'sets' e.g. how many more children are there with dark hair than with fair hair?
- Data handling: pose a question; collect data (perhaps about growth, eye/body colour, favourite food/TV programmes etc.); represent using block graphs, bar charts, pictograms, Venn diagrams, Carroll Diagrams etc. (Perhaps suggest a relationship between light eyes and light hair?) Analyse the data; interpret results.
- Enter and access data on computer database e.g. 'Our facts'.
- Measurement: using parts of the body as non-standard units of measurement e.g. handspans. Discussion about the need for standardized units.

Language
- Topic work could centre upon each child making a book entitled 'My Life' in which photographs, artwork, etc. could back up the text.
- There is a good opportunity for children to write autobiographically as a free-writing exercise. They might predict what they will be like as adults.
- Children can explore their feeling through story – 'How would you have felt if it had been you?'
- The writing of diaries or journals over a short space of time can help to focus thoughts and feelings.
- The writing of 'Who am I?' riddles in which more and more information is given about a child can be fun.
- The 'Guess Who?' game is a good exercise in the (logical) process of elimination.

Science
- A good opportunity to learn and label the parts of the body (see Art).
- Investigation into body growth: create hypotheses/questions; observe and measure; interpret findings (e.g. why has Hannan grown more than Wayne?)
- The Senses: 'How do we find out about things? 'We can hear, see, smell etc. 'What can we do . . .with our eyes, with our ears etc.' Devise and carry out 'fair' tests to measure qualities of taste, hearing etc. Sensitive discussion of handicap. 'Feely boxes'.

Technology
- Design a machine which can prepare and serve your favourite meal.

Geography
- Likes and dislikes about features of the local area. The children may like to draw up plans for improvements to the playground or write letters to the local council suggesting small improvements to a local square.
- 'Where do I live?' Local maps and a child's route to school could be drawn – 'what do I see on the way to school?'

History
- Personal time-lines: what a child was like/did at various stages of his/her life from birth.
- Make comparisons with children from a different era e.g. the Victorians.

Art and Craft
- Portraits and self-portraits using different media.
- Life-size paintings of the children can be created by working in pairs and drawing round one another. These can be cut out and displayed. Parts of the body can be labelled (see Science).
- Making Masks (see Drama).

PE/Dance/Drama
- Exploring body movements: 'how many different ways are there of moving an arm?'
- 'Work out a dance to tell the 'story' of your life so far.'
- Drama: acting out 'things that make me feel . . . sad/happy/angry etc.' Masks help to break down inhibitions.

Music
- 'What do my ears tell me?' (see 'Senses') e.g. volume, pitch, timbre etc.
- Songs

Multicultural/RE./Health
- If there are children who have different cultural heritage and/or religions, these can be celebrated.
- A 'talent' day could be organized when teachers and children can share some of their talents (eg ballet, skate-boarding, things done to help others etc.) Discussion of the talents of handicapped people (the Paraplegic Olympics?)
- 'Keeping Safe': dangers around the house; talking to strangers etc.